HOW TO GET A *Woman* TO HAVE *Sex* WITH YOU

If You're Her Husband

Second Edition

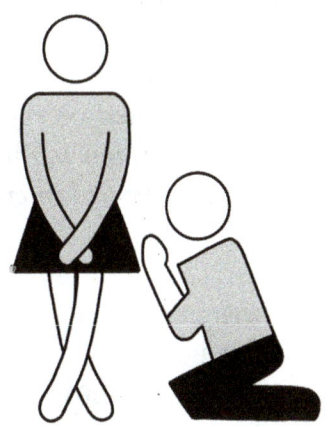

Stephan Labossiere

Atlanta, GA

How to Get a Woman to Have Sex With You If You're Her Husband.

Second Edition
Copyright ©2012 Stephan Labossiere.

All rights reserved. *Printed in the United States of America. No part of this book may be used or reproduced in any manner whatsoever without written permission except in the case of brief quotations embodied in critical articles or reviews. For information, contact:*

Allwrite Publishing
P.O. Box 1071
Atlanta, GA 30301
www.allwritepublishing.com

1. Marriage 2. Self-Help 3. Relationships 4. Life

LCCN: 2012920851
ISBN: 978-0-9844931-9-7

First Printing: November 2012

Dedication

It's important to me to witness people leading authentic lives enriched by mutually satisfying relationships. I believe that God puts us here to experience joy and love, and when we find the person who captures our hearts, it is God's will that brings us to that person. Many times, we experience negative circumstances that harden our hearts and force us to fear the very thing that can heal us, love. We lie to ourselves and to each other. This breeds more negativity, miscommunication and destructive relationships. Therefore, I dedicate this book to bringing an end to the battle of the sexes and breaking down the communication barriers between men and women so that we can all start being real with each other and, in that realness, not be afraid to love each other.

Contents

Preface i
Acknowledgements v
Introduction vii

CHAPTER 1
Happy Woman = Happy Man 1
    The Rules 4
    The Outcome 16

CHAPTER 2
That's the Last Darn Time 21

CHAPTER 3
A Connection Deeper Than Sex 31

CHAPTER 4
You Gotta Do More Than Just Lick It 43

CHAPTER 5
Have a Date With Her Body 55

CHAPTER 6
Spice Up Your Sex Life 71

CHAPTER 7
You Need Someone Else to Answer to 83

About the Author 91

Preface

So many people ask: What made you write this book? My answer is that many married couples are struggling with their relationships. Some couples put on a great act that everything is okay, but in reality, they feel empty and unhappy. Not everyone feels comfortable going to a therapist, and others have no other physical source to which they can get great guidance. I have always been that guy who people open up to and come to for advice. Thus, becoming a certified relationship and life coach seemed natural to me. This has allowed me to delve deeper into relationships and help many people over the years to overcome obstacles and move their relationships in a better direction. I know that this is my calling, and this book is the first step toward reaching a broader audience to spread the message of better and more fulfilling relationships.

I was once married, but for all the wrong reasons. If I were then, who I am now, I would not have taken the same route. I have personally experienced how a lack of understanding a woman and, more importantly, a lack of appreciation for the beauty of marriage can do so much damage. Fortunately, I grew up in a home where my parents were married for 37 years until my father died. Though it was not perfect, it showed me what commitment to marriage is all about. My three sisters are all happily married. As the only male amongst my siblings, my sisters always have confided in me about their relationship issues.

Having been married does not necessarily teach you what you need to know. If that were the case, more married men would have come to understand women better by now, and we know that this is simply not the case. I can honestly say that in the process of getting closer to God is where I truly began to see things differently. This is how I came to really understand the needs and desires of women. God basically trained me about marriage and not marriage itself.

Truth be told, I think it would be very difficult for a married man to write this book. When you are in the midst of the back-and-forth battle of a relationship, it is very hard to see things clearly and unbiased. This is the same reason why people will talk to a counselor, a church authority, or a friend. They need an outside opinion to help point out things that they may not be looking at because they are too caught up in their own feelings, issues and desires.

If you are in a relationship in which your sex life is lacking, you can choose to not listen, but it will not help change your circumstances. A lot of married men would like to simply believe that since they are married, they should be entitled to sex when they want it and how they want it, at all times. Being caught up in that way of thinking will not allow them to look deeper and find a solution or even realize that there is a problem.

Although this book revolves around improving sexual relations, in essence, it helps teach us how to have a better relationship. I have put the focus on the men because I believe the responsibility falls more on us to be better in our marriages. It isn't that I am letting women off the hook, and I believe there is plenty they could do better. However, when I speak to a person about his or her issues, I always focus on what that individual can do better, and since I am speaking to the men, then that is where I have placed my focus. I can only hope that you will be open to all that has been said, and that you will be willing to at least try a different approach in your marriage. Ultimately, you are married, so you might as well do all that you can to make it the best it can be.

I am certain that if you take heed to what is said, you will be able to see an improvement in your overall relationship, as well as your sexual relationship with your wife. This isn't easy for most men, but with commitment to improvement, adequate time, and persistence, it will become more natural for you to consistently do things that will be beneficial for your wife and ultimately you.

Stephan L.

Acknowledgements

I'd like to thank my friends and family for their support and feedback while I worked to complete this book. I'd also like to thank everyone who has allowed me into their lives, trusting me to listen and give advice in the hopes of learning and growing in their relationships. A special thanks to my mother for her guidance, love and support in raising me to be the man I've become. I hope to make her proud everyday of my life. Lastly, but most importantly, I thank God for all that I am and all that I have. My life's experiences and blessings could not have been realized without my spiritual devotion to God and the blessings that come with God's love.

Introduction

Somewhere in this world, a man is waking up right now. He looks over his shoulder to see his wife asleep beside him. He stretches and yawns, and then he proceeds to get up and make his way to the bathroom. As he flicks the light switch on, he can't help but notice his bathroom is filled with feminine products. He then does his business and heads to the sink to wash his hands. As he finishes up, he looks in the mirror, wipes his face with his hands, and at that very moment he thinks, "What the hell did I get myself into?"

That's right, folks. Almost every man has that moment where he asks himself that question, wondering why in the world he got married. It is a sad and unfortunate thing, but it is a reality. Now the reasons can vary as to what makes the man question his decision. Maybe it's because he wishes they could talk more or maybe he doesn't feel emotionally fulfilled. (I would laugh right now, but I'm sure there are some men who really feel this way.) Maybe it's her inability to support him the way he needs, bad cooking, not cleaning enough, being overbearing, and the list can go on and on. I'm sure, though, that if we did a survey, one of the biggest reasons that men wish they could turn back the hands of time is LACK OF SEX! I capitalized those words to make sure that any women reading would truly get that this is urgent. If you don't give your husband some action soon, his "friend" might just wither away and turn to dust. Really, this is an important issue that a lot of marriages are facing, and to be honest, most men have just accepted that it's a part of the program. They have utterly given up on trying to figure this out. They honestly start to believe that their wives just don't like sex, and there is nothing they can do about it. Well, I'm here to tell you there is hope. This book holds the key, or shall I say keys, to unlocking this mystery. Before I get into showing you the light at the end of the tunnel, I think there are some important things you're going to have to realize first.

Fear is Powerful

Okay, so first thing you do is get a camera and catch your wife in an unflattering situation. Then you give her an option: sex or this footage hits YouTube. I'm joking, of course, and I am not trying to insinuate using scare tactics will get the results that you want. Though she may be prone to using fear tactics (i.e. withholding sex, threatening to poison your meals, talking you into a coma), it is not the route you should take.

Whether you realize it or not, a lot of women are in constant battle with their fears. She is scared to open up and completely let you into her heart. Some of you may be saying, "But I thought this was just about sex?" Here's a newsflash: sex for a lot of women isn't that simple. We can debate whether it should or shouldn't be, but the fact remains this is the reality in many situations. Her fear of exposing herself and, therefore, putting herself in a vulnerable position is neither appealing nor comfortable to her. She may have been through emotionally traumatizing experiences or simply have a negative view of men based on what she has seen or heard.

The truth is that a lot of women believe that it is inevitable that a man will do something to hurt them, so they will take whatever necessary pre-cautions to protect themselves. Being her husband does not exempt you from this belief, so don't think you're different. Just understand this issue so that you may approach things properly and delicately. You can never personally eliminate her fear yourself; it will be on her to do that. You can, however, help to decrease or completely eliminate it over time. This book will help you with some of those aspects, but you must have patience.

 Rome Wasn't Built in a Day

I understand that we live in a society that wants results fast. We want everything to be easy, and when we have to put in work, some of us shy away. Well, nothing that is built to last is built quickly. It takes time. Now, I'm not saying you can't get some very fast results, but if you want to change the way you and your wife consistently operate sexually, then understand it may take some time for her to come around completely. There will be some cases where a few adjustments here and there will get things going in the right direction immediately. Then, there will be others with issues so deep that it will take a lot of working through issues to start to see some improvements.

Consistency is the key in all cases. If you only "act right" when you want some, then she will pick up on that and will purposely deny you of your desires. Trust me, if you remain consistent with your "correct" actions, she will soon become consistent in hers. Do not forget, she is still a woman, and that means she is processing and analyzing things on a level that you have no understanding. This could lead to her attempting to test how genuine this new approach is, which brings us to the next point.

 The Words Coming Out Her Mouth Are Just Distractions

Contrary to what you may believe, your wife is very smart. She may play dumb, but she pays attention and is analyzing a lot more than you think. She knows you very well even though you would never guess that by judging how she treats you at times. With that said, when you begin this process, there will be some wives – the majority – who will pick up on this different approach you're taking. She will want to see how genuine you are or if she thinks that this is all about sex. She will then purposely make things more difficult for you. She will try to throw you off by saying and doing certain things just to test you. Don't fall for it! Stay focused and learn how to look past a woman's words to truly understand what she is really saying and what she is trying to achieve.

My hope is that as you read this book you will be able to do things genuinely. Regardless, don't let her take you off track because this mission is too important.

Forgive and Forget Because this is the Dawn of a New Day

One of the biggest obstacles you will face is letting the past linger in your mind. You're so used to being turned down that the slightest resistance makes you wave your white flag. You think because you previously came to the conclusion that she doesn't like something, then you shouldn't bother with it. Please throw that all out the window because you will only delay your progress. Even if she starts doing what she usually does, let's focus on approaching it differently. Try to approach it differently to see if you get different results.

There is a lot more to your woman than most of you probably know. Focus on this new beginning. Look at your marriage like a computer that possibly has caught a virus and is no longer functioning the way you would like. You're now going to re-format the hard drive, which is erasing everything on it for those of you unfamiliar with this terminology, and re-install everything. Now some of you may be saying, "Well, isn't that like saying to get a divorce and get a new wife?" Nice try, buddy, but the answer is no because it's still the same computer. You're going to remove all the bad habits and start fresh with a new approach, and you can't succeed at doing that if you're still living in the past.

So with that said, now you're ready to learn what it is

going to take to get your sexual lives back in order. Not to mention, if you truly take heed to all you're about to read, I can guarantee you will get even more than just an enhanced sexual life, you'll get an enhanced marriage.

Chapter 1

Happy Woman = Happy Man

"There is no greater invitation to love than loving first."

St. Augustine

I once attended an event that consisted of a panel discussing relationships. A young woman in the crowd raised her hand to ask a question, saying, "Why is the focus always on what a woman needs to do?"

She essentially wanted to know why there wasn't any discussion on what men needed to work on other than simply being a provider and protector. Panel members agreed with her notion that this truly is the case, but nobody seemed to have an answer for her.

When you think about it, this concept holds true in a lot of places. You always find seminars and information on what women need to do and work on. Even in many churches, there seems to be more emphasis and responsibility put on women to step up. I think the reason is very simple. The average man has no clue on what a woman truly needs or, in some cases, even wants. So, if he does not know, how can we expect him to go out and spread the word to others as to what they need to know? On the flipside, women know the answer, but the average woman is not willing to give a man or men in general the directions to her heart. Frankly, they do not trust men with that kind of understanding because they believe most will just abuse it and find some way to hurt them in the end. So, we create a situation where men are left frustrated and confused, and a lot of women are left unhappy and unfulfilled. This, in turn, has made marriage look like a miserable choice that most will still attempt because we are programmed or socialized to do so.

The reality is that marriage can be a much more rewarding experience for many if we just took more time to understand each other. A quote by Oscar Wilde says, "Women are made to be loved, not understood." How can you properly love that woman and give her what she needs if you do not understand her? Your perception of love and how to give it may not be the same as hers.

The Rules

I'm sure you have heard, "Happy woman equals a happy man." Even if you haven't, it is truly a theory to live by if you're a man looking to have the best relationship you can have with a woman. Unfortunately, a lot of you may not truly understand what makes a woman happy. You also may be thinking, "Why can't the equation be in reverse: Happy Man = Happy Woman?" Well, first let me address the latter of the two. A happy man does not always equal a happy woman simply because our needs are simple. A lot of men can be happy as long as they are being fed, left alone, and getting some booty on a regular basis. It can be really that simple, whereas the woman's needs are more complex, at least from a man's point of view. It is always easy to find a woman who fulfills those simple needs of her husband and keeps him happy while she is secretly miserable. On the flip side, when a woman is truly happy—not pretending or lying to herself and everyone else, but truly happy—in her relationship, there will almost always be a happy man by her side.

When a man taps into a woman's emotions, stimulates her mentally, and fulfills her in ways that may seem so ridiculous to us men, she will naturally start to reciprocate the things you need and desire. She will take joy in it, and it will only add to her fulfillment. Women have a natural instinct to nurture, so once you're able to tear down all the walls that life has created, you will receive more than you bargained for.

Now let's address the other point. Most men do not know how to truly make their woman happy. You're probably reading some of the things I have written and saying, "How the hell do I tap into her emotions?" "Do I really want to deal with tapping into her emotions?" "I'm hungry," and "I could really go for some sex right about now." All of these are understandable, but if you want the best out of your marriage, then you want to pay attention and understand what you need to do to make her happy so that you are

Chapter 1. Happy Woman = Happy Man

happy. So, here are a few rules to remember:

1. *Security* – Most, if not all, women want to feel secure. Part of the reason women look to get married is to bring a sense of security and stability to their lives. Unfortunately, a lot of men fail on how to strengthen that feeling but, instead, do things to damage it. Security has a lot to do with trust, so you have got to learn to build the trust she needs to feel secure with you. Being open and honest about everything goes a long way in that department. So, for example, don't hide your phone or walk out of the room when you have a phone call. Behaving like that can easily raise an issue and create a trust issue. If you know you have nothing to hide, then behave accordingly, and it will help her feel more at ease.

Also, we, men, have a tendency to not let women into our lives enough. Your woman shouldn't have to hear from someone else your dreams and aspirations, or any current business dealings. Someone else should not be telling her where you're at when you should have already told her. I know that may bother some men because you may feel like you're being punked or something. GET OVER IT! You're simply creating an environment where your woman feels valued in your life and doesn't have to question things all the time because she will already know what's up, and that really helps with her feeling secure.

2. *Communication* – Yeah, yeah, yeah, I know everyone gets told all the time that communication is the key. Well, it is people, and that's why you keep hearing it. Like it or not, your woman wants to talk. Yeah, it may be a bit long-winded and include a bunch of unnecessary details. It may be of no interest to you, and you would rather drive over your own foot than to listen to her. Hell, you probably don't even hear words anymore, just "womp, womp, womp, womp." Still, you need to listen. Taking some time out of your day to fulfill her need to be heard won't hurt you. Ok maybe it will a little, but it's for the best. Try creating some time each day that you set aside to really talk to her. Ask her how her day was and actually try to focus and listen. The last thing you want is for her to ask, "What did I just say?" and you can't give an answer. Remember, communicating with her is what she needs, and when she is satisfied, you're more likely to get satisfied.

Also, communicating is necessary to let her know what you're feeling and thinking. It helps to provide some of the emotional security she needs (as we discussed earlier) and helps to nurture a better connection between the both of you. Never leave it up to a woman to try to figure you out because Lord knows what she will come up with and drive herself insane thinking about it. Her theory will then be thrown at you, and you could both land yourselves in a mental asylum, county jail or hospital, depending on the type of woman you have. So do both you and her a favor by opening up the lines of communication and being more willing to listen and share.

Side note: If she is extremely long-winded, maybe you can get a timer and put a limit on the conversations. If she goes past her limit, she either has to immediately engage in the sexual activity of your choice or receive a small electrical shock. She cannot choose to be shocked more than twice in a row, and she must act like she enjoys the sexual act. I hope you realize by now that I'm just joking and this suggestion should not be taken seriously. Moving along...

3. *Non-sexual intimacy* – Some of the men are probably saying, What the hell is that? Does that even exist? Or better yet, What's the point of that? Non-sexual intimacy is the act of being intimate and affectionate with your wife without leading to sex. It does exist, and it is very necessary for your wife. Even if you were blessed with marrying a naturally sexual firecracker, she still has a need and desire for non-sexual intimacy. Women do not want to feel as if they are just your piece of meat to be used at your discretion. They want to feel loved and desired, and when intimacy always leads to sex, then it completely ruins their hope of being more than just a sex toy to you. Now understand that non-sexual intimacy for a woman not only includes physical aspects like touching, caressing, hugging, etc. It also includes quality time alone, talking, and other ways of connecting. She may simply want you to sit next to her and watch TV with her for an hour or so. As pointless as that may seem to us men, especially if her show of choice is on Lifetime or some other depressing channel, it is still something you should and can do to fulfill her needs and make your relationship better. You could take a walk with her in the park, cuddle with her, or give her kisses and affection all while not expecting sex out of the deal. It will make her feel wanted and loved. This will definitely help push the relationship in a better direction.

4. *Reliability* – One thing that's very important to women, but I don't think gets expressed enough, is having a man they know they can always count on, a man who knows how to take care of things and truly be the man of the house. When she knows that you will take care of things and do it in a timely and efficient manner, it adds to her trust and feeling of security. It removes an added layer of stress that she will have if you're a good-for-nothing type of person who can't correctly handle the simplest of tasks. The less she has to worry about, the more she can focus on doing the things that you need from her. Granted, if you are working like crazy to take care of the household, you will have less time to take care of some of the other things. If that is the case, then you just need to talk to her and come to an agreement on how things will be handled. Maybe you two can agree on her taking care of some of the major household duties like cleaning the house and laundry, while you handle less time-consuming tasks like the trash, car maintenance, and household repairs. If you are the one who pays the bills, make sure they are paid on time because if there is no running water in the house, there will be no water-producing (sweat, people) activity in the bedroom.

Now, I am all for compromise and getting input from your wife about whatever issue is on the table. I am also going to remind you that you are the man, and you need to handle yourself as such. No woman wants a punk! She doesn't really want a yes man for a husband. Some may claim they do, but trust me, after a while, you will look weak and lose her respect. Learn to be a good leader of your household, which means listening to your partner but still taking the lead and making decisions when necessary. I am not telling you to run a dictatorship, but you still need to be viewed as the head of your household. Again, some women may fight your attempts to take charge when necessary, but if you stand your ground, she will not only respect you on also be very turned on by your assertiveness.

Bottom line, be the man of the house she truly desires you to be. If you say you're going to do something, then do it and do it correctly. If you don't know how to do certain things, then learn how rather than letting them fall on her shoulders, unless it's absolutely necessary or she wants to handle it for you. Allow her to feel secure in knowing that she has nothing to worry about because you're on the job and you know how to handle your business at work and home.

5. *Financial Security* – Before any women reading this start to say, "I don't need a man for his money. I can get my own," let me just say, BLAH, BLAH, BLAH! Look, I fully understand that in today's world, there are plenty of women who make a good living and can provide financially for themselves, so much so that they even become the main breadwinners in their marriage. I also understand that money may not be the most important thing to a woman, and it really shouldn't be. Let's get real, though, the last thing a woman wants is to have to carry a man financially for an indefinite amount of time. Sure, he doesn't have to be rich or wealthier than his woman, but he does need to be able to hold his own. Women may be okay with it at first, but it will get old and eventually create an issue. Some women will start to lash out and belittle their husbands because she makes more or all the money. He may start to feel insecure, which can lead to many issues. I'm not saying that there aren't people who have had beautiful relationships in which the woman makes the money and the husband stays at home with the kids. I'm just saying that it doesn't work for most, and many women expect their husband to lead in that area. Again, by being a good provider and holding down the household financially, you relieve your wife of unnecessary stress, which in turn leads to better things for you both.

6. *Sexual Prowess* – Although I would stress that sexual satisfaction for a woman is more mental than it is physical, that doesn't mean we can just overlook the physical component to their sexual pleasure. We have to understand all that comes into play when satisfying your woman. Let's first address size. Some women say it's not important, and some women say it is. The truth is, unless you are abnormally small (I will leave that up to you and your woman to decide), then God has given you enough to get the job done.

If you listen to women talk, they complain both about small men, as well as men that are too big or big for nothing. Of course, if you're working with a bigger piece of equipment, then it will allow you to hit some spots a smaller man may be unable to reach. Rest assured, there are still ways to please your woman even if you aren't as "blessed." Take into consideration that a recent study has shown at least 70 percent of women don't reach an orgasmic climax through intercourse alone. So knowing how to properly stimulate her clitoris (i.e. orally, manually, sex toys, etc.) can be more important than how big you are or are not. Some of you may still be bothered by your size deficiencies, but most of you have no excuse as to your lack of stamina in the bedroom. I think we can all agree that a woman wants a man who is capable of going for a long time, and that two minutes of loving just won't cut it. Not that she wants an all-nighter every time you do it, but you should be able to put in the overtime when needed because let's face it, you may need to put more time in to allow her time to reach an orgasm.. Whether it is size, stamina, or technique, there is a lot a man can do to combat performance issues. Both eating right and exercising play a major role in improving your sexual effectiveness. Taking the time to learn her body, as we address in Chapter 5, and implementing different techniques can also go a long way in bringing her the sexual satisfaction she needs, which will increase her ability to sexually satisfy you as well.

7. *Making Her Feel She's #1* - I know what you're thinking: If I married her, isn't that enough to show that she is number one in my life? NOPE! Just because you slap a title on a woman, it does not give her the complete feeling of being number one. It does help, and it may be a quick fix, but it's temporary. Making her feel as if she is at the top of your totem pole (after God, I hope) is going to be a constant process. Understanding and implementing the first six things on this list will help your wife feel like she is your one and only, but realize that she may have some additional ways that can help you reinforce that belief. This includes always introducing her as your wife, especially to other women, as well as showing her affection and love when others are around, especially in the company of other women (notice how I keep repeating that). She does not desire to simply be your number one lover, but rather the number one woman in your life.

For you mama's boys, cut that umbilical cord and stop putting your mother before your wife. I understand she gave birth to you, took care of you, and all the other beautiful things mothers do. However, I can guarantee you that if your mother was in your wife's shoes, she wouldn't be too happy with being put second either. Your wife's position in your life needs to be honored and respected. Not to mention that if you are a Christian, the Bible clearly lays out the order of priority to be God, your spouse, kids, and then work. So there really isn't a valid excuse spiritually or logically not to put your wife first. If you are not capable of doing that and have yet to marry, then stay unmarried until you can get that right. Some may feel that's harsh or irrational, but I am telling you now, your inability to put your wife first will leave her unfulfilled. If she is unfulfilled, there is a great chance you will be too.

Side note: I just have to add that I hope you will come to realize that your wife needs to be treated like a queen. She is to be loved and cherished for the blessing that she is. She should be placed on the highest pedestal possible (under God) and given the utmost respect. However, if she ever comes at you wrong and disrespectful, kick that pedestal right from under her ass, look her in the eye and remind her you are her husband and she will respect you as such! Don't mistake treating your wife correctly for being run over. Just had to give that reminder. Please don't literally kick a pedestal right from under your wife because that would really, really hurt.

 ## The Outcome

These seven rules are just some general ways that you can focus on what, I believe, are core needs for most women. Of course, your woman may have a few things that will be different, but you will have to learn those things and implement them. Still, if you can get the above seven right, then you will be in a greater position to leverage regular sex.

After reading these rules, some men may be thinking, "Why does it have to be all about her? What about me? If she did right by me, then I would have no problem doing these things." Although I understand your position, it's that mentality that's keeping you from having a better marriage. This isn't about giving 50-50. Honestly it isn't even about giving 100-100. It's simply about giving 100, meaning your only focus should be about what you're doing and not what she is doing. If you worry about her side of the bargain, chances are you will find reasons not to give your all and handle things properly. You have to learn to put your best foot forward regardless and trust God that she will fall in line, and believe me, she will.

If a woman can't bring herself to give you what you need when you are truly giving her everything she needs, then she has issues that are way bigger than you. If this is the case, you may have to consider more serious action, such as counseling. I am all for couples counseling, but I believe that it becomes extremely difficult to address personal issues as a couple. Couples tend to go into counseling and focus on the other person's wrong-doings until it becomes a competition of finger-pointing. Also, if the counselor assigns an assignment for the both of you to do individually, it becomes very easy to pay more attention to your partner fulfilling his/her assignment, and the second he/she doesn't, you may have the urge to throw it all away, including any progress made during counseling. So, I believe that individual counseling is necessary first or during the timeframe that you're doing couples counseling. A lot of the issues you have often stem from things that existed well before your marriage and were never properly addressed. Some of the same problems you are currently facing are simply manifestations of those old issues. So consider re-evaluating yourself and getting yourself right so that you may be better-suited to make improvements in your relationship.

Truth be told, most men are not fulfilling their women. They are doing some things right, but still aren't getting the whole picture. Some of you may claim that you did this and that, and you still didn't get what you were looking for. Well, for one, you probably did what you thought would make her happy rather than really finding what she knows will make her happy. Your perception is not always her reality, but if you take the time to get into her world and see things through her eyes, you will be well on your way to making her a very happy woman and soon find yourself a very happy man.

Summary

- *Security* - being open and honest with her will builds the trust she needs.
- *Communication* - she wants to be able to talk to you and you actually listen to her.
- *Non-sexual Intimacy* - she doesn't want to feel like all she is to you is a sex toy.
- *Reliability* - she wants you to be a man, not just in the bedroom.
- *Financial Security* - everyone likes that peace of mind, but if you can't provide financially, make sure you're providing domestically.

- *Sexual Prowess* - if you want more sex, you have to learn to give better sex.
- *She is #1* - other than God, nobody should be put above her.

Chapter 2

That's The Last Darn Time

*"Appreciation is a wonderful thing.
It makes what is excellent in others
belong to us as well."*

Voltaire

Let's say one day you decide you want to do something special for one of your kids or family members, like send them on a special trip. You take the time to set everything up, and you make sure it's done in a way that you feel she would like. You're very excited about everything that you have planned and how she might react to it. So the day comes and you give her the surprise, but the reaction is very bland. Or maybe she does have a good reaction initially, but as soon as she gets back from the trip, the first thing she talks about is why you don't send her on trips like this enough. What if she only talks about some of the less stellar parts of the trip without mentioning the good parts? Maybe she even hassles you about planning another trip immediately? That would probably make you upset, maybe miserable, probably frustrated, and you would more than likely not want to make the effort ever again.

Well, men, this is how some of your wives feel about you and sex. They feel unappreciated for their efforts. They feel as if it's never good enough. They think, "Why bother when I get no appreciation when I do give in to his needs?" (Note that she feels like she is "giving in.") Where do they get this idea? Simple, it comes from you. When you complain about not getting it enough, you hurt your cause. When you catch an attitude or lash out when you don't get it when you want, you hurt your cause. When you insult the quality of her sexual performance, you again hurt your cause. Taking a negative or critical approach to solving your marital sexual issues has never really worked, so why keep taking that route? It may get you the response you're looking for in some cases, but it will never last.

Now I'm not saying that you shouldn't be allowed to express a desire to want it more or for it to be better. You should always be honest, but your delivery must change. Before you can even do that, we must return to the issue of appreciation. The first thing you must learn to understand is that a lot, if not most, of you have wives who aren't fully enjoying the experience of sex on a regular basis with you. Unfortunately, women don't receive the consistent climax that we as men do. I mean, if you kept going to the gym for months and didn't see many results, would you keep working out consistently? No, you probably would become less consistent, have to drag yourself through it, or just flat out not even bother. Well, it's the same thing for her, and you must begin to understand that so you can start making the necessary adjustments.

With that said, you have to learn to appreciate every time the two of you are intimate. Appreciation breeds production, so remember that. When you truly show somebody you appreciate something, and not only with words, you make them want to do it again simply because it makes them feel good to be appreciated. Everybody likes to get something for his or her effort, especially when something is done exclusively for the other person's benefit. It's about reciprocity or a mutual exchange of privileges. For some, all it takes is seeing the other person happy in order to feel rewarded. One way or another, whether it is a physical reward or an emotional one, we like to get something back. So you have to learn to give that appreciation, which will, in turn, motivate her. Many of you may ask, "What's the best way to show how you appreciate her sex?" Well, I'm glad you asked because here are some things you can do:

1. *Don't complain about the lack of sex* - If you want to express your desire for more sex, do it as a compliment, not a complaint. Learn to say something about how you just enjoy being with her or how you enjoyed it so much and you can't wait to go at it again, etc. When you complain, you will just turn her off, and it will work against you.

Even though some women may give in to your complaining and give you some "shut the hell up" booty, this is a temporary fix and definitely not the way to go. Furthermore, this giving in sex is usually unfulfilling, so

Chapter 2. That's the Last Darn Time

really what's the point?

"Getting off" will only get you so far, leaving your wife sexually deprived, which certainly does not help your cause. Case in point, if your kids complained and complained and complained, you would get annoyed – maybe even smack the crap out of them – and your desire to please them would diminish. Find better ways to communicate your desires, and it will surely help your chances. I'm not saying that this will instantly get you more sex because there is more to it then that, but this is a much better approach then complaining. This may not be an instant fix, but it is one that will serve you better in the long run.

2. *Don't insult her skills* – Listen, I understand if your lady really isn't that good in bed or to your liking. I understand if she doesn't do half the things you would like to see her do or have seen performed somewhere like in an "adult movie." (I am not promoting porn, just acknowledging the fact that many of you watch or have watched it and possibly admire the skill set exhibited). In some instances, you may have a woman that takes that insult as a challenge, and consequently, she steps up her game. Typically, however, insulting her will not motivate her, but instead discourage her. This isn't football practice where insults can, at times, motivate a player to step up. These are women, and it's usually best to encourage them.

Also, while engaging in sexual acts, be responsive and express when you like what she is doing. Moaning, grunting or giving her a nice smack on her ass are all ways to show her that you enjoy what is being done. You can also throw in eye contact or the way you grab/hold/touch her during that moment.

All of these things can make her feel good, motivate her to get more into it, do more or engage in the act more often. If you just lie there unresponsive, she won't want to bother. I'm not saying you have to talk dirty (unless she likes that, then you should), but at least show her you're into it so she can get more into it as well.

❸ *Be the man you need to be* - The best way to show her your true appreciation is to handle your business overall. When you are the man she is looking for, it will motivate her to open up more and be the woman that you are looking for. Handling your business means she can rely on you, which is very important to a woman. How would you feel as an individual if you couldn't rely on your partner? If the simplest things you asked her to do and she brushed them off or handled them improperly, you would see her as ungrateful and unappreciative. That is exactly how your wife would feel if you treated her that way. Handle your business, and she will let you handle "the business" in the bedroom.

Now there may be other ways, depending on your woman and what she may be looking for, but the examples above are always where you need to start. If your issue is that you truly can't wrap your mind around this concept or can't seem to be genuinely appreciative, you're going to have to start making a conscious effort to do it. You may have moments when you just want to lash out or a complaint just comes out. However, you just have to catch yourself, correct your actions, and commit to improving your approach for the next time.

The concept of appreciation is very simple, and it can be achieved on a consistent basis. Just put yourself in her shoes or think about how you would want appreciation for your efforts. I'm sure you may feel unappreciated about some things, and it probably discourages you too. So keep showing appreciation and give it some time, and you will start seeing some great results.

Summary

- Show some appreciation. It breeds production.
- Don't complain about a lack of sex. You can talk about it, but focusing only on the negative will not be very effective in fixing the situation.
- Don't insult what she does. An insult is a quick way to get her to not do anything you're looking for.
- Be the man you need to be. A great way to show appreciation is by always putting your best foot forward.

Chapter 3

A Connection Deeper Than Sex

"Love is supposed to start with bells ringing and go downhill from there...and as we stayed together, the bells rang louder."

Lisa Niemi

There is a huge misconception that problems in the bedroom mainly get solved in the bedroom. I have even seen some shows and read articles by certain relationship experts that actually push this idea. However, it does not work like that. It might work very well for men but definitely not for women.

We could only hope it was that simple, and, in a few cases, it can be. Don't be fooled, though, I did say "few cases." Sex is more mental and emotional for a woman than it is physical. Think about it, your actions are fairly redundant. Your stroke has not changed much, and you only use a few variations in your approach to foreplay. So how is it that one night it's great and the next week, it's far from satisfying to her, as she lay there thinking about what she needs to do tomorrow, waiting for you to get off? "What's the difference?" you ask. The difference is where she's at mentally and emotionally now. Or as I like to say, "Open her mind and her legs will follow." You can also remove the word mind and insert the word heart and the principal remains the same.

Basically, if you lack an emotional, mental, and spiritual connection with your wife, then you will also lack countless hours of great sex as well. What's happening outside that bedroom has much more to do with what's happening in it

Chapter 3. A Connection Deeper Than Sex

than you have ever realized. We, as men, get so caught up in life's distractions and our own needs that we completely lose sight of getting in tune with our significant other to truly understand what she needs and desires. Let me add that the redundancy of your acts in the bedroom doesn't help either, but we will address that later in chapter 6.

Now, once you begin to truly understand the principle that there is more to it than just plain ole sexual desire, you will then begin to remove the blindfold and see things more clearly. It's not completely your fault that you have been blind this whole time. Women themselves helped to put that blindfold on you whether intentionally or unintentionally. I'm sure they will argue that point, but that's just part of the process to keep you in the dark. They want you to figure things out on your own. Women are not going to reveal all there is to know about them even if it means throwing out mixed signals that will only keep you lost and confused, as most of us men are.

With all that said, the big question is how do we as men connect with our wives on a level that will satisfy them and give us that extra bump in bedroom activity? Here are a few things you can do, but I must warn you that you will like some tips less than others.

❶ *First thing* is talk to your wife! Open your ears and your mouth, and she will open hers in more ways than one. I realize that I already mentioned communication in chapter 1, but I feel the need to repeat it and drive the point home some more. When people say communication is key, it really is. When your wife feels like she can talk to you and you listen, it will make her feel more comfortable with you. You can't just sit there and say "uh huh," "for real," "that sounds great," or "you talk too much". Even if you don't say the last one out loud, you're probably thinking it, and that needs to be removed as well. I know most men don't care for long conversations that we deem pointless, but do it because you love her and because it will help create a better connection that will improve many aspects of your relationship.

❷ *Second thing,* stop being so judgmental about all women! Yes, I said all women. What you fail to realize is that your judgmental comments about your woman or any woman at all that you make in front of your wife affects her mentally. Women are constantly thinking, and they remember nearly everything you say (whether they allow you to believe that or not). I don't care if she makes similar judgmental comments because sometimes that's just a trick to throw you off and see where your head is on a particular topic. Now, I don't want anyone to lie. If you truly feel the way you do about something, then you go with that, but remember, it's not what you say but how you say it. I do want you to try to be more open minded so that you can truly start to look at things differently, which will in turn help your marriage.

Here's an example: you're sitting with your wife and watching a movie. In the movie, a woman gets freaky with some guy and lets him (insert freaky act here i.e. put his finger in her butt). She may be watching this thinking how she would love to do that same freaky act, but she's afraid of you judging her. So what she does is either flat out asks you what you think about that or, worse, she sets you up first with a judgmental comment on her end and then sees how you respond. Since you're a man, you know that your words may be used against you in the future, so you may try to pick the right thing to say, at least what you think is the right thing, which it's usually not.

So what are your possible responses?

A. Whether you truly feel this way or you're just saying what you think you should, you end up insulting the woman in the movie, saying things like she is a hoe, skank, slut, etc.

B. You show that you have no issue with that freaky act and see nothing wrong with what the woman did.

Now, you would think it would end there, but some women will actually continue to push the issue just to see if you will change your answer. She will even start to insult you and make it seem like you're so disgusting. You are still better off being open minded about it because if you answered with "A," you just ensured that the chances that your wife will do that same freaky thing with you are very, very slim. Why would she feel comfortable doing the same thing you passed judgment on another woman for doing? She won't do it to you, but unfortunately, she may still turn around and do it to somebody else. If you answered with "B," then you increased your chances, barring that you don't say anything too stupid between now and the next opportunity to make that happen. This brings me to the next thing.

3. *Though it may be difficult for some,* you're going to have to learn to think before you speak. I'm not saying you need to analyze your every word or lie to her. You just need to be more aware that what is coming out of your mouth can completely turn her off or land you in the dog house. Comments and questions such as: "Have you gained some weight, honey?" or "You should try to look more like her," typically do not go over well with women, so be more mindful. It only takes one stupid comment to talk yourself out of some booty, so choose your words wisely, men. In fact, compliment and encourage her as much as possible.

4. *Next, a little more interaction* with your wife would help. This means spending time doing something she likes to do outside the bedroom. I know what you're thinking, "Isn't talking to them and living with them enough?" Nope, it isn't!

How many of you have heard your wife say, "We never do anything together"? For those of you who nodded or raised your hand, and for those of you who have yet to hear it, women say it because it's important to them. You can't have a connection if everything you do is disconnected. Find something that you can do together to help nurture that connection. Some of the things they may ask us to do with them will seem pointless, such as going shopping or watching a cheesy show together. She needs it to feel connected, so why not compromise and find a few things you can do with her?

A woman doesn't want or like for everything you do with her to be about sex, although I realize that I am telling you to accept this fact on the premise of trying to get you more sex. This is why you need to learn not only to embrace interacting more with your wife, but also to find ways to actually enjoy it. Although that concept may seem impossible for some of you, I believe there has got to be some way to make it work. If she feels that everything is always about sex, then it devalues her as only being there to fulfill your sexual appetite, and she wants to be more than that. Sometimes women just want you in the same room as them or just sit by them and relax. Again, it will seem pointless to us, but to them, it is of great importance.

5. *This may seem less obvious* than the other suggestions, but women like men because of a man's perceived strength. This is one reason many women are immediately attracted to men in uniform or athletes, and why most women are turned off by men who are lackadaisical or lazy. Married men should remember this fact and attempt to support their wives in household chores and repairs. This is especially true if she works full time and/or has children. A woman will have a hard time making love in bedroom where the roof is leaking, for example. Fix the roof or get it fixed without her saying a word or at least too many words, and watch how responsive she will be to you when you need a fix. If she feels overwhelmed with the children, for instance, take the kids off her hands when you can. When she is tired, you cook or take her out to eat. In other words, you be her strength when she is weak or discouraged.

One thing that I feel is a big thing you can do is to pray together. At times, we are at our most vulnerable when we pray. Thus, allowing your partner to share in your spiritual outpouring to God, especially since you are one in His eyes, can go a long way in establishing and maintaining a connection.

So the bottom line is to learn how to get in tune with your wife outside the bedroom, and watch how everything in the bedroom improves.

Summary

- A connection outside the bedroom will help create or maintain a better connection in the bedroom.
- You have to communicate; it helps nurture a connection.
- Don't be judgmental; it will only push her further away from you.
- Do things with your wife to also help nurture a connection.

- Support your wife in household duties and do extra if she feels overwhelmed.

Chapter 4

You Gotta Do More Than Just Lick It

*"For a man to feel loved, he needs to make love.
For a woman to make love she needs to feel loved.
So that's why the foreplay, the romance, is so much
more important to a woman."*

David Weir

Now I know what you're thinking, this chapter is going to be about the good stuff, such as kissing, touching, licking, and all the other little freaky and kinky things you can think of. Well, get your mind out the gutter. Actually, keep your mind in the gutter, but let's try to realize that there is so much more to foreplay than that. Let's start out by looking at the definition of foreplay, courtesy of Wikipedia:

Foreplay: is a set of intimate psychological and physical acts between two people meant to create desire for sexual activity and sexual arousal.

It goes on to say:

Any act that creates and enhances sexual desire in a sexual partner may constitute as foreplay.

So in plain English, if it can turn your woman on, then it's foreplay! That should be real easy, right? (I will allow you a couple of minutes to laugh, vent, or go into a moment of silence about how wrong this statement is.) I will now rephrase the statement and say that it really should be easy, but in reality, the majority of men don't know what turns on their woman. Yes, you know a few spots on her body that really do it for her. Maybe you have a pet name that she loves to have you call her. You might even have a few extra tricks here and there that you are aware of if you're lucky.

Unfortunately, you may think you know all there is to know, but there is so much more you have yet to touch (pun intended). Not to mention, you probably have used the same methods so many times that now they just don't pack the same punch they used to in the past. You can only grab her breast or smack her butt so many times before the act loses its flavor. You're going to have to add other things to it. So let's look at what you need to understand about foreplay and some of the things that turn a woman on or can help you learn what turns your woman on.

RULE #1: *She isn't going to tell you everything!*

If you have the audacity to think that you can just walk up to your wife and ask her what turns her on, then you are sadly mistaken, buddy. Sure, normal, sane people understand that explaining what you want will give you a better chance of getting what you want, but how dare you assume your wife is that rational. She is a woman! And I say that with a lot of love and respect.

Women feel that since you are with them, you should have the desire and the ability to figure things out for yourself. She might drop some hints if you're fortunate enough, but no matter how much you sit and talk with her, she isn't going to spell everything out for you. Another reason she won't tell you everything is because she is concerned you may judge her and look at her differently if you realized how much of a "freak" she really is. Trust me, most of your wives are much bigger freaks and much more sexual than any of you realize. You are just going to have to start trying things on your own to find out what she is really about and to get her to open up.

RULE#2: *Foreplay is not limited to right before having sex!*

We, men, have got to understand that women are not like us, and therefore, it can be a longer process to get her in the mood. The 10 minutes or less of messing around pre-sex isn't always going to cut it. Look at it like this, men are like standard light switches that you can just flick on or off (though we pretty much just stay on 24/7), and women are like the switches with the knobs that you have to turn to make the light bright (a very slow turning knob). There are a variety of ways you can get the process started early, such as sending her naughty text messages and emails, rubbing her leg while in the car, doing something nice and meaningful earlier that day, public displays of affection (i.e. deep kiss, holding hands, rubbing her lower back, etc.), and so forth. Believe it or not, and this may surprise you, cleaning the house could really get her going, especially if you're typically not the type to do so. Let her come home one day and see you washing dishes (If you're physically fit, let her catch you with your shirt off cleaning the dishes for a bigger impact), and watch how her eyes fill with a lustful desire to "put it on you."

So with all that said, understand that you have to start planting seeds as early as that morning or even the day before. This doesn't mean that you should give her a warning in advance that you're going to want to have sex. Instead, you can start doing the little things in advance so that by the time you get to the pre-sex workout, her knob will have already been turned, and you just have to finish it off to have her light shining bright. So do things like compliment her, saying sexy things to her, but just don't do anything stupid to counteract the effect. I know we don't like to think ahead, but if you want more action, you better put on your military hat and do a pre-emptive strike.

RULE# 3: *Going Down On Your Woman Is Not Just For Before Sex!*

This topic covers more than just foreplay, and I feel it is something that is extremely necessary to say. I am aware that plenty of men may already understand this, but I have come to realize that there are still a lot more men who do not. Going down on your wife should not just be a part of the "pre-game meal." I mean, it's good that you're doing that, and it's a nice thing to do to get things warmed up, but it should not stop there. You should learn to throw it into the mix and do it every now and then during sex. Or even better, after you have climaxed and you need your 5-15 minutes to "get back up," then do it during that period so she can still be into things and be pleased while she has to wait. It also will enhance the sexual experience for her, in most cases, which all works in your favor.

Some of you are probably thinking, "Get back up?" Well, if you're one of the men who are "one and done," then I need for you to get it together. One round is typically not going to be enough for your woman unless you are really amazing in that one round, which again typically is not the case. Learn how to go at least two rounds, thus giving yourself a better chance at satisfying your woman.

Another thing you should consider doing is exercising

if you currently are not. Some men get comfortable with their bodies being out of shape, and then wonder why their woman is not as willing to have sex. Not to mention that being out of shape hurts your performance as well. So take some time to hit the gym and reap the benefits it can provide for your performance, as well as her desire to engage in more sexual activity.

RULE #4: *Man Up!!!!*

Many men seem to underestimate the desire of a woman to want a man to be aggressive and assertive at times. Sure women want to be made love to and handled gently. You definitely need to learn how to be more sensuous and patient, but don't fall into a belief that this is all she wants. Almost all women, if not every woman, wants you to "knock it out the frame" sometimes if not the majority of the time. Seriously, she wants you to take control and be "manly." So even with your foreplay, displaying that passion and assertiveness in a controlled manner can go a long way to getting her very turned on and ready to go. Notice I said in a "controlled" manner. What that means is you're not trying to literally hurt her (unless that's what she is into, and I'll leave that between you, her, and the chains and whips you have stored in your closet), but you are trying to take command of her body.

Look at it like this: there is a way to throw your woman up against the wall that is sexy, and there is a way to do it that cracks her skull and sends her to the ER. Learn how to not do the latter, and you will be fine. Take in consideration that every woman's threshold for what is enjoyable aggressiveness will vary. As always, take time to learn what works well for your woman. Also, aggressiveness isn't only displayed physically, but verbally as well. So speak with confidence and assertiveness, and watch how those panties may just slide off all on their own.

RULE #5: *It's Not A Race; It's A Marathon!*

I totally understand that it is very hard to be patient while performing foreplay. As a married man, you're just so anxious to get to the main event because 1. You don't know when you will get it again, 2. Because you waited so long to get it you're extremely anxious and 3. You're trying to make sure you get it before this crazy woman either changes her mind or finds some other reason not to continue. So again, it really is understandable, but if you want to make things better in the long term, then you still have to learn to fight those concerns and take your time.

Trying to rush through foreplay will, most of the time,

leave your woman unfulfilled. Also, if she isn't in the mood, she will not be as into it as she needs to be, which takes away from how enjoyable the experience could have been for the both of you. I do acknowledge that there are times where foreplay is unnecessary. Also, the amount of time you need to spend on foreplay will vary from woman to woman. That is where you have to really learn about the woman you're with so that you will know how much works for her and when it's necessary. Regardless, you have to be patient and put in the necessary work.

If you were really hungry and had to cook some meat, wouldn't you wait until it was done and cooked properly, knowing that will almost guarantee a very delicious and fulfilling meal? Or would you rather just eat it raw out of the freezer because you couldn't bear to wait? If you happened to choose the latter of the two, I am really going to need you to reevaluate your level of patience and sanity.

Remembering and practicing these five rules will definitely put you on the right track to more consistent, enjoyable sex with your wife. Never forget that foreplay is an ongoing process and not limited to things you do physically. Your woman may be turned on by the smallest things, and taking the time to find them out, will pay off big time.

Summary

- Foreplay is any act that creates and enhances sexual desire in your partner.
- She isn't going to tell you everything, so you just have to learn to push the envelope and test things out sometimes.
- Foreplay is not limited to right before having sex. Sometimes you have to start early to get your woman in the right mood.
- Going down on a woman is not just for before sex. Find some time while having sex to please your woman in this way.
- Sometimes you have to really take your time to please her correctly.

Chapter 5

Have a Date With Her Body

"To attain such ecstatically erotic levels of intimacy and enjoyment in your sexual life, you need to understand her body and what brings her pleasure."

Raymond Ehoma

So you've been married for however long now, and you figure you know your wife pretty well sexually. You have gotten her to achieve an orgasm - or at least you think you have - and scream wildly at night. You know her spots and the different ways to turn her on. You know what kind of woman you've got, and you're confident you can satisfy her, right? Wrong. I'm here to tell you that you don't have a clue. You may have some knowledge of your woman, but you are far from knowing everything.

Rarely do men take the necessary time to find out everything. Even now, there is still more to discover with the woman you're with sexually. Some men haven't pushed the right buttons; others have yet to push the envelope. Now, you've heard me say that communication is the key, and in most cases, it definitely is. However, when it comes to the bedroom and women, you can throw that principle out the window for the most part. Why? Because she isn't going to tell you everything, no matter what you want to believe. I don't care how many conversations you've had with her, she just isn't going to flat out say everything that she is willing to do between the sheets. Why? Because women are freakin' crazy, that's why! They refuse to make things simple! They are just complicated for no reason at all! In all seriousness, they are crazy (just kidding, ladies), but that's not the reason even though that's the explanation we men like to default to at times.

The truth is, in addition to the fear of being judged by you, your woman wants you to figure it out for yourself. It's so much better to her when you can pull things out of her without her having to say a word. When you just know what to do and she never has to tell you or give you instructions. She might tell you a few things here and there, just not everything. Some of it she may not completely know herself, and never had a man to truly try to help her find out. Which leads us to the next predicament: How the heck are we supposed to know what she wants if she doesn't tell us?

Here, my friends, comes my solution to this problem. The first thing to understand is that this is going to take focus and attention to detail. To accomplish this, you must make this all about her, and put your personal desires for that night aside. Okay, I will predict that about 95% of men reading this book just closed it and are cursing my name after my last statement. So let me add for those brave soldiers still reading, the process as well as the result will be very rewarding for you. TRUST ME! So, here is an example of what you can do. You pick a day, and please don't make it her birthday or any other special occasion. This is its own special occasion and will have a much greater impact when it's done separately from already celebrated days. On this day, your focus needs to be all on your wife and her body. Most of the time, we do romantic things for our wives because we hope to get ours in return that day. Today, throw that out the window. I know that's hard, but, again, trust me. This will pay off for you big time!

How you want to set the mood is totally up to you and your knowledge of what your woman likes. Universal things that will help are:

1. *A clean house* – a dirty place can be a mood killer, as well as serve as a huge distraction. I know some men are capable of having sex in a dump if it came to it, but that's not going to work for most women.

2. *If you have kids*, leave them with someone she trusts. So you can't leave them at your boys' house who has no clue about kids. Neither can you leave them with a complete stranger who's a friend of a friend who she has yet to get acquainted with. If you put them in a place she isn't comfortable, she won't be able to think straight and stay focused on what's in front of her, which will lead to her feeling uneasy, making several calls to check on the kids, etc.

3. Resolve any lingering issues before this day - you have to show her you care about how she feels emotionally, so that she will let you "feel" her physically. If she is still pissed off because you made a less than tactful comment about her weight recently, then she is just waiting to throw that back in your face, which could ruin this night. So address issues when they happen, and don't just brush it off like it's no big deal because to her, it is a big deal.

4. Sometimes, you need to warm her up to what's going down that night. As mentioned in chapter 4 about foreplay, you have got to start early. Send some nice texts or an email. If you talk to her, which you should limit that day, make sure to compliment her or say something sexy.

If you are not too sure what to say, try leading with something about how good it feels to be next to her. You can also mention that no matter how many people you come across; she is still the most beautiful woman you know. It is usually safer to start with non-sexual comments and throw in more erotic comments later, such as how you can't wait to see her so that you can make her feel really good. Notice I just put a general "make her feel good." You do not always need to be specific, especially on a day like this. Leave it up to her imagination to wonder what you may have planned. The suspense is good, and her process of thinking about what you may have in store will help in getting her ready for the night. The main thing you want to do when you make these comments is keep the focus on her. You do not need to say you are anxious to see her so that she can do the things you like. Do not come off selfish and worried about your satisfaction; just worry about hers.

Let me add that, depending on your woman, you may want to go right to the sexual comments. You should actually switch it up from time to time so that it is not the same approach every time. By doing this, you will at least get an idea if she is in the right mind frame to handle any of that day. If her demeanor gets prickly, you can scratch the whole operation and leave it for another day. Other than that, customize it based on her likes and turn-ons.

One more thing that's universal: smell. If you already wear cologne, good; if you don't, go buy some! One suggestion: Stop choosing cologne based on what smells best to you. Yes, you should like what you're wearing, but this really isn't for you. It is for the woman. So find out what she likes or get the opinion of a woman at the store. I have never purchased cologne without a woman's opinion, and my cologne has always gotten compliments. In addition to cologne, make the house smell nice, nothing too overbearing, just something nice, simple, and light.

So now we have the house clean and smelling good, the kids are at a trusted location, no lingering issues, and you even smell good. Here is the next thing to remember, and it's a big one: DON'T SAY A WORD! That's right, keep your mouth shut. Men, we have a tendency to say something stupid (in their eyes) and mess it all up. I could attempt to list examples, but honestly, what may sound okay to one woman could be the biggest turn off to the next. This is why limiting what you say that day will, at the very least, decrease your chances of pushing the wrong buttons.

If communication is really necessary, leave simple notes for her to read, but just don't open your mouth. None of the notes should flat out say what you're about to do to her other than possibly letting her know it's all about her right now. This could be extremely important for some of you because you may have a woman that has a built in defense mechanism. The minute she sees all this, she starts thinking, "Oh, he just wants to get some," and she may shut it down before it really gets started because she isn't "in the mood" or "happy with you." Letting her know it's about her and only her may help you get through her first line of defense.

Back to the communication issue, your woman isn't stupid. You don't have to verbally express to her what's going on, and if she is that slow, then Lord help you. I should also add that women are like men in the sense that they don't all operate very well on an empty stomach. So, please make sure that either she has already eaten or you can start this off with a light meal, nothing heavy.

At some point, you obviously take her into your bedroom or any area of choice as long as it's somewhere you know she is comfortable, and begin to slowly please her and explore her body. Now she again may throw up her defenses and think that you're just trying to get some. So, leave your pants on to prove that this is for her and not you. Secondly, if necessary, this is where you can open your mouth and give a reminder that this is all for her and not you.

In an attempt to prepare you for any negative feedback, I have to say that if anything goes wrong or she just refuses to take part in this, then don't get upset, don't act out, and don't go into detail about what you were trying to do. Just leave it alone and go about your business, remaining friendly and cordial. This will only throw her off and work completely to your advantage. Not to mention, you should always try to handle things in a positive matter because it's always best.

Chapter 5. Have a Date With Her Body

Now, since it's all about her and you're not going to concern yourself with your needs, you should be able to take your time. Pay close attention to how she reacts because that will tell you what she likes. A woman can fake many things, but she cannot fake simple impulse reactions, such as her back arching, a sudden clinching of your body, and so forth. Also, pay attention to how she moans. If something you do triggers a moan, but she is holding back from letting it out too much, then you're on to something. Focus on what you're doing at that moment, and see if her moan intensifies. The key is focusing on what you're doing and then doing it with no reservations. When you're hesitant, you are half-stepping, and that's never good. You have to do it with confidence, because if you think you're not doing well, there is a good chance she will think the same.

In addition to the usual spots, try unconventional places to see if you get any reaction from that. Let me rephrase, try everything; explore every inch of her body. You will be surprised at the spots that may get your woman going. Understand also that there are good spots, and there are "the spots," meaning a lot of places that you tend to try may give her a really good feeling or turn her on, but there are specific places that drive her wild.

At no point do you ask her for permission to do something; just do it! When you give your wife an option to decline your offer, you simply increase the chances of her saying no. You allow her time to process any and every reason she can come up with as to why she should decline. It could simply be because she is concerned about how you may view her afterward. It could also be that, at that moment, she remembers something you did to piss her off, so she views this as a good time for payback. The possibilities are endless when you are dealing with a woman, so do not open that door. Now, I am not saying to just out of nowhere ram your finger in her butt (I do not have a fetish with this. I just like using it as an example), but I am saying there is no need to forewarn her. Certain things you can just hit her with, and others you need to ease into. When doing something you have never done before and you're unsure whether she will like or be comfortable with it, just set it up correctly. Get her feeling good first and caught up in the moment of pleasure, and then BANG! Blindside her with this new freaky thing. Even if she never thought she would like it, if it feels good and she is already in the mood, she will continue. Otherwise, you can do it in a way that gives her time to react and stop you. Trust me, if she doesn't like it, she will block it, but if she lets you continue, then don't question it. Just focus on her reactions. Keep mental notes because these are things she isn't going to tell you; you just have to figure them out and remember. She may be willing to communicate more about it once it has actually been done.

This whole night should last no less than an hour. In all fairness, that time can be adjusted depending on the woman and how things are going. I know it seems like a long time for basically foreplay, but remember, this is all about her and she could lay there forever.

If she tries to take control at some point or starts trying to please you, then you aggressively – in a good way – take that control back and let her know with your actions that this is for her and only her. If she shows you she wants to be penetrated, then so be it, but even that should be done with a focus on her and what she wants. Other then that, it should remain at foreplay the whole time. Now, I said it should last no less then an hour, but if she takes longer then that to have an orgasm, then you better just keep it going until you get her there or she insists on stopping – hopefully because she is satisfied, and not because you lack skills. When you're done, don't go asking if she liked it, she will let you know without a doubt. At least wait until the next day if you must ask.

Just remember, though, you don't have to—or may not get to—do everything in one night. In this way, you leave room for more nights like this and more chances to explore, which is good for both you and her. You may surprise yourself by finding spots that even she never knew existed.

So what have you just accomplished with this day? Well, my friend, this one night just got you more sex and more love in the future. For one, you should know your woman and her body much better after this night, therefore allowing you to be more satisfying to her in the future. That will, in turn, get you more sex. You also showed her that you can be patient and resist being selfish to make it all about her. She will appreciate and love you for it very much and that will, in turn, get you more sex. If she loves you, she is going to want to return the favor. Note: If she wants to return the favor, it will be when she wants to give it to you, not when you want it. So, don't start asking her when is your turn or you will decrease your chances of getting it.

With all that said, you should not only do this one time in your life and that's it. This should be done every so often, and you should always try to add a new element to it. As much as you may accomplish in that first time, you probably still have more to learn about your wife, so you have to keep it going. Things can change sometimes, so you have to always stay up on any new developments in her sexual desires. I know some men are going to say, "Well, how about our day? When do we get ours?" As I stated earlier, just relax because trust me it's coming! [Put the disclaimer in the previous paragraph about waiting for her to return the favor here.] You've just got to realize that the more you make it about her, the more she will give you what you desire and then some.

The reality is that men don't consistently take enough time during our sexual encounters. You can't keep leaving her dissatisfied and expect her to keep giving you what you want. Since you know you won't be able to be consistently patient during sex, then give her a whole night of your attention and patience afterward to help balance things out.

I will end this chapter with an analogy I like to use: If sex is a job, then as men, we get paid every time we go to work. Women, however, don't always get their checks. Thus, most of them don't want to come to work anymore or are consistently absent because they aren't getting paid. Many of you just don't have it in you to make sure she gets paid every time, so how do you offset that? You increase her benefits, and giving her nights like this can definitely make her a much happier member of your organization. It's the least we can do, and it will definitely get them to come to work more often.

Summary

- Set aside a night to get to know her body better.
- This isn't about you; it's about her.
- Leave no part of her body untouched.
- Pay attention, and get more in tune with her desires.
- Be patient with the idea of reciprocation

Chapter 6

Spice Up Your Sex Life

"Couples who describe themselves as loving, trusting and caring complain that their sex lives have become dull and devoid of eroticism."

Esther Perel

Instead of hearing oohs and aahs or your name screamed out for something other than what you did wrong, the sounds of your woman snoring is probably all you're getting at night. One of the biggest problems is this: The sex has gotten boring. It's a snooze fest, and it gives her no motivation to come back for more. I do understand that after years of marriage, things can get like that at times. You figure, "How much variety can I have when I am having sex with the same person for the rest of my life?" You feel like you have tried different things, and there isn't anything left on the list. Well, for one, that's complete BS. You probably have done many different things with her, but there is always more that you can do and haven't done.

The problem is you're either not thinking hard enough or you're overthinking it. Sometimes a small change can really help. It's not always about trying something you've never done before, but simply doing more of something you usually don't do enough and learning how to do it better. When you have fallen into a routine way of having sex, then doing something that you have done before but maybe not done in a long time, is still a good way to spice things up. We tend to focus on the sex itself rather than ways we can switch it up, which is a good start, but stop acting like you've tried it all. Let's discuss a few things that you can do to help enliven things:

1. *Positions:* "The Dirty Dangle," "The Couch Canoodle," and "Standing Tiger/Crouching Dragon" are just a few positions I'm sure a lot of you have never heard of. You can search the internet or find various books with a plethora of different positions to try, and I bet that most of you haven't even done half of them. Heck, you probably have not even tried a third of them. You can't really think that doing missionary all your life isn't going to lose luster at some point. Even if that just happens to be her favorite, there is still so much more to explore, and it would work in your favor to give it a shot. You may want to assume that she just won't go for this, but little do you know how much she wishes her husband wasn't so boring in the bedroom.

Trying different positions are great and all, but how about also trying to actually be good at them? A position isn't as boring or as ineffective when it's actually being done correctly and hitting the right spots. How about having a night every now and then - which she does not always have to be aware of in advance - where you only do the atypical positions? Don't try to do everything in one night. Take your time to focus on how she likes it, and you'll definitely start making things more interesting in your bedroom.

2. *Location:* I realize some of you are thinking about how you have already done it in so many different places. However, have you done it in all these different places with your wife? Just because you had an old girlfriend that checked a bunch of things off your to-do list in terms of locations, does not mean you can't reset that list when it comes to your wife. It also doesn't matter if you have done it everywhere in the house before with your wife. And if you haven't, then you have more to work with. Let's say, though, that you have hit every spot in the house, but for the last few months or even years, it's always been in the bedroom. One day getting down in the kitchen again will still help to spice things up.

Also, get more daring, and do it somewhere crazy. I say at least once a year, you pick a really crazy place to do it and hope you do not get arrested or traumatize a young child for life – cue in the laughter, please. Like I mentioned in the previous chapter, you don't always need to ask for permission or clearance. Just give it a try and have a backup plan for making the situation a good one if your original intentions fail.

3. *Predictability:* The element of surprise! That's right. You need to learn how to be a little less predictable. That woman knows your every move and exactly what you're aiming for when you execute it. She can read you like a book – like one of my books, which you can always find out more about at *www.stephanl.com*. I was due one shameless plug. Don't judge me.

Her being able to read you does not help at all. In fact, it works against you in the bedroom. I don't care who you are, we all fall into redundant routines, and after being together long enough, she will be able to see right through you. Trying the things mentioned above will help, but you still need to hit her with some other curve balls. Think about what you usually do when you want to try to have sex, and now completely do it differently. If you have a habit of trying to have sex on Saturday night, then this Saturday, just spend time with her and don't even utter the word sex. If you consistently attempt to have sex in the morning before work, then use that time one day to help with the kids or make breakfast, and again, don't even utter the word sex. If you tend to offer doing a favor for her as a setup for trying to get some, then offer her favors and look for nothing in return instead. Whatever it is you usually do, DONT DO IT! And preferably, replace it with something nice. I don't care what she says or does, you are completely throwing her for a loop, and that's a good thing. The less a woman has you figured out, the more interesting you become, which is a definite advantage to you.

In addition to doing things differently, be spontaneous. You can never be predictable when you're spontaneous. Hit her with something when she least expects it, and do something she doesn't think you would do. Again, asking for permission or getting some form of verbal clearance in advance is not always necessary. Plus, the minute you do that, you take some of the spontaneity out of the action.

So let me give you an example of how you can completely have her mind spinning by doing things against the norm and be spontaneous all in one session. (Disclaimer: If this example isn't your cup of tea, well learn to drink it, buddy! If you want to get more out of your wife, then you're going to have to step your game up!) So let's say you have the house all to yourself, and if you happen to have kids, they won't be back for an hour or so. Some of you may complain that this is unrealistic because you never get time alone. However, that is still no excuse to not find a way to make this a reality. Now back to the example. You come home and your wife is washing dishes. She is wearing something that gives you easy access to her you-know-what. By "you-know-what" I am referring to her "vagina" aka "love box" aka "heaven between her thighs" or whatever you like to call it. You greet her, and the first thing you should do is help her with the dishes. Don't be mistaken, this isn't about helping around the house per say, but when you do something like that, it's a good way to soften her up, and for some women, it can be a major turn on. Since you probably don't usually help with the dishes like this, you already have her mind going, wondering what you're up to, and that's a good thing.

Next, accidentally drop a utensil on the floor right behind her. After you go to pick up the fork, start kissing her on her leg. If she asks you what you're doing, you either don't answer or tell her don't worry about it. Now I can get into little details, but the goal here is for you to "go down" from behind while she stands there bent over the kitchen sink. If she shows you a little hesitation, just take control because if she really wanted you to stop – and she doesn't – she would make it clear.

Now, there are two different ways to approach this at this point. You can either handle your business until she reaches climax, or if you know her body well enough, you can push her to the point where she is ready to climax, and then stop. Whichever road you choose, when you're done, you simply get up, give her a smack on the ass, a kiss on the cheek, and then walk away. Yes, just walk away! I know what you're thinking; you did all that just to walk away? Do understand what you have just done? If you don't understand, here is the breakdown:

1. That was completely spontaneous to her and probably nothing she would expect from you, so that alone has her extremely turned on and excited.

2. After pleasing her, you didn't even try to get yours, and that has her head all messed up because it was totally unpredictable.

3. To add to all of that, you just walk away like it was nothing, so she has no clue what is going on. And, trust me, she isn't going to let it end there. So what will ensue is she will probably sexually attack you at some point before the kids do get home and give you all you could ask for without having to say a word.

I must warn you that women are very smart and catch on quickly. You can't keep pulling this stunt and think she isn't going to switch things up on you. Some may even be strong enough to resist the urges the first time you pull this on her. To counteract this, you have got to keep changing your approach. Also, let's say you do it for the first time, and she comes to you but then resists. Please understand that she is burning up inside, and she is simply trying to keep her composure. Your mission is to break her, which you will do by continuously being nonchalant, but still doing subtle things to turn her on. Don't talk about what you want, or don't ask for anything. If you speak about sex, let it be a story using other people. If she tries to call you out on what you're doing, just play dumb. Eventually, she will break, and everyone will be happy.

So there you have it, a few ways you can turn that boring sex life of yours into something spectacular and much more interesting. Is there more you can add to this list? Of course, there is, but as always, that will depend on your woman. For instance, not every woman cares to engage in activities using toys and such, but I have given you some basic principles (i.e. spontaneity, etc.) that you can use with any woman. These are things that anyone can do, and they aren't as hard as you may think. Being redundant in your ways will lead to a redundancy in her turning you down and getting less action. I do realize that a lot of men are going to say, "Why am I going to go through all of that just for one day of sex?" You lack vision, grasshopper, because a day like this will lead to much more than one day of sex. It can help set up many more days. You just need to be consistent and focused so that you, as well as your wife, can reap all the benefits.

Summary

- **Positions** – There are a plethora of different positions, and I'm sure you haven't tried them all.
- **Locations** – It doesn't always have to be some place new, but it shouldn't always be in the exact same place.
- **Predictability** – After being with you for so long, she knows your every move. Whatever you usually do, do it differently and throw her off.
- **Spontaneity** – everything doesn't need to be planned. There are a lot of ways to liven things up. You just need to take the time and put some thought into it.

Chapter 7

You Need Someone Else To Answer To

"The husband should give to his wife her conjugal rights, and likewise the wife to her husband."

1 Corinthians 7:3

You're probably wondering how in the world this man who just spoke about all this sexual stuff is now going to speak about God? Well, it's simple. God does not have an issue with sex in a marriage. Can you find a scripture that speaks against sex in marriage? Some would argue about oral sex and sodomy, which I leave up to others to debate, but I have yet to find any general issues about sex in a marriage. So why do we act as if we shouldn't go there, or that it's impure, as if the Lord will strike us down for getting a little freaky with our partner with whom we have made a life commitment? Not only is it okay, in my opinion, but it is also a beautiful thing that God wants you to enjoy with your wife/husband. Some Christians tend to believe that sex should only be used to make babies and not for physical pleasure. Not only do I believe it should be used for physical pleasure as well as having babies, but I believe it should also be used as a time to bond and connect with your partner.

If you're married, then should you not be free to fulfill your husband and wife sexually with no worries? I do not believe that God has asked us to wait on being married to fulfill our sexual desires, only to then put a bunch of limitations on what we can do with our partners. Could I be wrong? Of course I can because I am not God, and I am imperfect just as we all are. I am simply sharing my belief on this topic.

Of course, if you are not spiritual and do not have a relationship with God, then these arguments will be viewed as irrelevant. If you do have a relationship with God, then I would encourage you to pray with your spouse and ask in prayer what might be okay for your marriage.

Some of you may be thinking, "I can't ask God if it's okay to handcuff my wife!"

I say, "Why not?"

Seriously, do you think he can't handle the topic? Don't you realize he is aware of way worse than that? He has pretty much watched one long "adult film" since the beginning of time, and I highly doubt He is surprised by anything at this point. If you're going to have a spiritual issue with something, why not be willing to take that issue directly to God?

This really isn't what this chapter is about, however. When you review this book and really break it all down, a man has a lot of work to do. Of course, to a woman, it's extremely simple, but it isn't to us. Not only is it a lot of work, but you're going to have concerns about whether or not it will work. What if I do everything in this book and this woman still doesn't find it in herself to please me and rock my world on a consistent basis? Well, that's exactly where

God comes in and one of the reasons this chapter is necessary. If you learn to put Him first, then it will help overcome those fears. This is not a quick fix, and you will still have your struggles, but it will help.

When you realize that your wife is a blessing and you should honor God by cherishing this blessing, then it removes the focus of your efforts from being all about her. You will start to do these things because it's what you should do regardless, and trust that your needs will be taken care of by God, who you are honoring by this approach. If you allow it to be all about her, then the second she does something to piss you off, you will revert back to your old ways. If you are making it about God, you will be hard pressed to find a valid reason not to continue doing things better. It does not mean you will become the perfect husband and never slip up. You will, however, become a bit more efficient in taking the better approach. In addition, by putting God first, you make yourself accountable to more than one person. Somebody once asked me if I ever cheat on my wife if I was guaranteed that she wouldn't find out. I answered with a "no," and they seemed surprised and skeptical. I went on to explain that though she may never find out about what I did, I still can't run from God, and there is no way for Him not to find out.

In short, you start to check yourself more when you know it isn't just about getting your wife upset. Because, truth be told, there will be plenty of days where you could care less if she gets upset. Heck, you may even intentionally try to get under her skin. Or you may even leave the toilet seat up on purpose late at night just so she can fall in. (Boggles my mind how some will not look before they sit.) With God first, though, you may think twice before you set her up to take a plunge in toilet water. You will also be hesitant to think it's okay if she is unhappy about something. This is when putting God first will remind you that there is someone else you have to answer to and you will not be able to make up a good lie to get past it.

When you decide to put God first in your marriage, executing all the tips to save your sex life become a bit easier. Again, it does not mean you are going to be perfect. It just means you will see the deeper purpose and have a better understanding for why this is all necessary.

Now with God as your first priority, I would also like to reiterate praying together. Have you ever heard the saying, "A family that prays together, stays together?" You should never forget it. It will help you and your spouse bond and form a deeper connection. It also gives your wife more security in the relationship, which only contributes to her being able to be all that you want her to be. Just remember that God wants you to be happy, so when you do put Him first, you can be assured that only good will come from that even when it does not seem like it right away.

Summary

- God does not have an issue with married people having sex.
- When you put your wife first, you take the focus off God, thus finding reasons not to do things for her when she upsets you.
- Making yourself accountable to Him will help you always put your best foot forward because it's what He wants from you, not necessarily your wife.
- God wants you to be happy, and your marriage to be great. So if you make Him your priority, you will help set the stage to receive those blessings.

About the Author

Stephan Labossiere is a man on a mission to help men and women experience more successful and authentic relationships. He knows firsthand how challenging the male and female dynamic can be and strives to bridge the communication gap between the sexes. The only male in a family of three older sisters, one of whom is his twin, Stephan has always held a deep fondness and appreciation for the way a woman's mind works.

Stephan grew up in Miami, Florida, before moving to and settling in Atlanta, Georgia. He has been an entrepreneur for the past 10 years and, most recently, has served as a relationship consultant to married and dating couples. This is his first book in a series aimed to break down the barriers and turn the battle of the sexes into nothing more than a pillow fight with a mutually pleasing ending.